Introducing Religions

Islam

Sue Penney

Heinemann

First published in Great Britain by Heinemann Library,
Halley Court, Jordan Hill, Oxford OX2 8EJ,
a division of Reed Educational & Professional Publishing Ltd

OXFORD FLORENCE PRAGUE MADRID ATHENS MELBOURNE
AUCKLAND KUALA LUMPUR SINGAPORE TOKYO IBADAN
NAIROBI KAMPALA JOHANNESBURG GABORONE
PORTSMOUTH NH (USA) CHICAGO MEXICO CITY SAO PAULO

First published 1997

ISBN 0 431 06642 6 hardback

01 00 99 98 97
10 9 8 7 6 5 4 3 2 1

ISBN 0 431 06649 3 paperback

01 00 99 98 97
10 9 8 7 6 5 4 3 2 1

British Library Cataloguing in Publication Data

Penney, Sue
  Islam. – (Introducing religions)
  1. Islam – Juvenile literature
  I. Title
  297

Designed and typeset by Artistix
Illustrated by Gecko Limited. Adapted into colour by Visual Image
Printed and bound in the UK by Bath Press Colourbooks, Glasgow

Acknowledgements

Thanks are due to Ruqaiyyah Waris Maqsood and Liz Powlay for reading and advising on the manuscript.

The publishers would like to thank the following for permission to reproduce photographs:
The Ancient Art and Architecture Collection p. 32; Kayte Brimacombe/Network p. 16; Circa Photo Library pp. 24 (below), 41; Sally and Richard Greenhill p. 7; Robert Harding Picture Library pp. 26, 33, 34 (left); The Hutchison Library p. 39; Christine Osborne Pictures p. 38; Peter Sanders pp. 8, 9, 10, 11, 12, 13, 15, 17, 18, 19, 20 (top), 23, 24 (top), 35, 36, 37, 40, 42, 43, 44, 45, 46, 47; Frank Spooner Pictures p. 31; Zefa pp. 6, 20 (below), 22, 29, 34 (right).

The publishers would like to thank Zefa for permission to reproduce the cover photograph.

Every effort has been made to contact the copyright holders of any material reproduced in this book. Any omissions will be rectified in subsequent printings if notice is given to the publisher.

Contents

MAP: where the main religions began

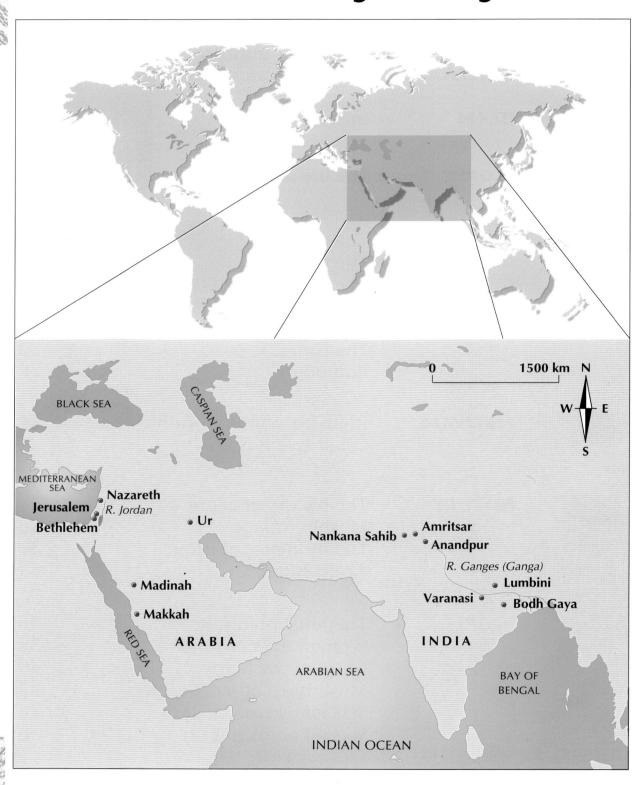

BLACK SEA

CASPIAN SEA

MEDITERRANEAN SEA

0   1500 km   N

W — E

S

Nazareth
Jerusalem
R. Jordan
Bethlehem

Ur

Nankana Sahib • • Amritsar
• Anandpur

R. Ganges (Ganga)

Madinah

Lumbini

Varanasi • • Bodh Gaya

Makkah

RED SEA

ARABIA

INDIA

ARABIAN SEA

BAY OF BENGAL

INDIAN OCEAN

TIMECHART: *when the main religions began*

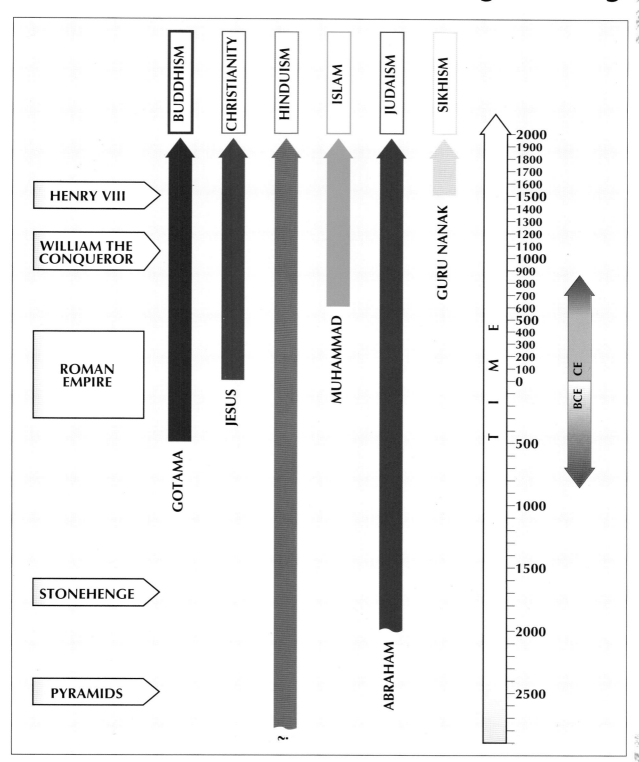

Note about dating systems   *In this book dates are not called BC and AD, which is the Christian dating system. The letters BCE and CE are used instead. BCE stands for 'Before the Common Era' and CE stands for 'Common Era'. BCE and CE can be used by people of all religions, Christians too. The year numbers are not changed.*

Introducing Islam

This section tells you something about who Muslims are.

Muslims are followers of the religion of Islam. Islam began in the seventh century CE in the part of the world we call the Middle East. Today, there are Muslims living in almost every country in the world.

What do Muslims believe?

Muslims believe that there is one God, whom they call **Allah**. They believe that Allah was never born and will never die.

Allah sees everything and knows everything. He made everything, and he cares about what he made. Because Allah is so important, people should **worship** him.

The prophet Muhammad

Muslims believe that Allah has always sent **prophets** to tell people how they should live.

Muslims believe that the last prophet was a man called **Muhammad**. He was born in a city called **Makkah**, and lived in the country we now call Saudi Arabia. Muslims believe that Muhammad was given messages from Allah. Allah's messenger was an **angel** called Jibril (also called Gabriel). The messages were collected together to make the **Qur'an**, which is the Muslim **holy** book.

Signs which Muslims use

Muslims do not use signs in the way some other religions do. Where a sign is needed for Islam, the one most often used is a star and crescent moon.

The star and crescent moon

Islam

Arabic writing at a mosque

The five points of the star are to show the five pillars of Islam (see pages 14–15).

'Peace be upon him'

Muslims do not worship Muhammad. He was not Allah, and only Allah should be worshipped. They do think that Muhammad and the other prophets were very important. So when Muslims talk about the prophets, they always add the words 'peace be upon him' after their names. This is sometimes written down as 'pbuh'.

The language of Islam

The language of Islam is called Arabic. Arabic letters are quite different from the letters used in English. Arabic letters need to be changed into other alphabets so that people who do not read Arabic can understand them. Sometimes different spellings are used for the same sound. For example, Muhammad can also be written Mahomet. Makkah can be written Mecca. The spellings used in this book give the sound which is closest to the sound of the word in Arabic.

New words

Allah the name for God which is used by all Muslims

angel messenger from God

holy to do with God

Makkah the city where the prophet Muhammad was born

Muhammad the man Muslims believe was the last prophet

Muslim follower of the religion of Islam

prophet someone who tells people what God wants

Qur'an Muslim holy book

worship show love and respect for God

The life of Muhammad

This section tells you about the prophet who began Islam.

Muhammad was born in about the year 570CE in the city of Makkah, in the country we now call Saudi Arabia. His father died before he was born, and his mother died when he was six. He lived with his grandfather, then his uncle. As he grew up, he helped his uncle, who was a trader. Muhammad became known for being honest. People called him Al-Amin. This means 'someone who can be trusted'.

When he was 25, Muhammad married a rich woman trader called Khadijah. It seemed that Muhammad had everything anybody could want. But he was not happy. He saw many things that were wrong with life in Makkah. Many people were getting drunk or fighting. They worshipped **idols**. Poor people were cheated by rich people. Muhammad began going to the hills near Makkah to be alone so that he could think and pray.

Muhammad's vision

One night, when he was praying in a cave, Muhammad had a **vision**. He saw an angel carrying a piece of cloth with writing on it. The angel told him to read it. Muhammad said that he could not read. In those days, not many people could read and write. But the angel said it again, and Muhammad found that he could read the words.

Then the angel said 'You are God's messenger'. Muhammad was very shaken by what had happened. He went home, where Khadijah comforted him.

The city of Makkah today

The Mosque of the Prophet in Madinah

After this, Muhammad spent his time teaching. Most people in Makkah did not listen, and he was unpopular. So in 622 CE, Muhammad moved to the town of Madinah. This move is called the **hijrah**. While he was living in Madinah, there were battles with the people of Makkah. Muhammad was trying to stop them doing what was wrong. At last, Muhammad and his followers won the battles, and the people of Makkah became Muslims. All the idols were carried out of the city. Muhammad went back to live in Madinah. He died in 632 CE.

New words

hijrah 'departure' – the name for Muhammad's journey to Madinah
idol statue made of wood or stone worshipped as a god
vision special sort of dream

The hijrah

The hijrah is the name given to the journey which Muhammad made from Makkah to Madinah. It took place in the year 622 CE. Muslims think that the hijrah was very important, because it was after this that Islam became successful. It was so important that the Muslim calendar begins from this year. The January to December calendar was begun by Christians, and goes back to the birth of Jesus. So Christians gave the years a number AD, which comes from words which mean 'year of our Lord'. Muslim years are AH, which comes from words which mean 'year of the hijrah'.

In this book, all years have a number CE (Common Era) which can be used by all religions. Muslim years are based on changes in the moon, not the sun, so they are about eleven days shorter than 'Christian' years.

The Qur'an

This section tells you about the Muslims' holy book.

Muslims believe that the Qur'an was given to Muhammad by the Angel Jibril. Muhammad learned the words off by heart. He taught them to some of his friends, who wrote them down.

Muslims believe that the words of the Qur'an are messages from Allah. They believe they should not be changed in any way. The Qur'an is written in Arabic, which was the language which Muhammad spoke. For worship, the Qur'an is always read in Arabic. Muslims who do not speak Arabic very well may have a copy of the Qur'an in their own language.

Copies of the Qur'an are always treated very carefully. When a copy is not being read, it is wrapped and put on the highest piece of furniture in the room. Before reading it, a Muslim will wash. Some Muslims learn the whole of the Qur'an off by heart. Muslims who have done this are allowed to use the title **hafiz** as part of their name.

This girl is reading the Qur'an.

Surahs
The Qur'an is divided into 114 parts, called **surahs**. The longest is surah 2, which has 286 verses. The shortest is surah 103, with only three verses. Apart from surah 9, they all begin with the words 'In the name of Allah, most gracious, most merciful'.

What is in the Qur'an?
Some parts of the Qur'an tell about things that happened. Others teach about how people should live and worship. The Qur'an does not teach that Muhammad was the only prophet. The Qur'an includes prophets like Abraham and Moses from **Judaism**.

It includes Jesus from **Christianity**. Muslims call them Ibrahim, Musa and Isa.

A beautifully decorated copy of the Qur'an

The Qur'an says that people changed what these earlier prophets had taught. So Allah made Muhammad his prophet and gave him the words of the Qur'an so that people would not change the teachings.

The Hadith

The **Hadith** are collections of the teachings of Muhammad. Muslims believe they are very important, though they are not as important as the teachings of the Qur'an, which came directly from Allah.

There are many books of the Hadith. Two of the most important collections are called the Hadith Bukhari and the Hadith Muslim. Muslims believe that the Hadith shows how Muhammad lived and taught, and what a good, wise man he was.

If Muslims have a problem in any area of life, not just in their belief, they will look in the Qur'an. If they cannot find an answer there, they will look in the Hadith. They will hope to find what Muhammad did in the same or similar situation when he was alive.

New words

Christianity religion of Christians

Hadith collections of the teachings of Muhammad

hafiz person who has learned the Qur'an by heart

Judaism religion of the Jews

surah one of 114 'chapters' in the Qur'an

The mosque

This section tells you about the Muslim place of worship.

Muslims believe that they can worship Allah anywhere. But they also have buildings used specially for worship. These are called **mosques**. (Sometimes the Arabic name **masjid** is used.) The most important time for going to the mosque is lunchtime on a Friday.

Outside a mosque
A mosque usually has a **dome**. There is also a **minaret**.

All mosques must have a place where people can wash, because Muslims always wash before they pray. This is nothing to do with being dirty. (It is explained on page 16.) So some mosques have a pool or a fountain outside. Modern mosques have washrooms with rows of taps.

Inside a mosque
There are no pictures or statues inside a mosque. This is because of the teachings of Muhammad, who said that people must not have them. He was afraid some people may begin to worship them instead of Allah.

Mosques are beautifully decorated with patterns and verses from the Qur'an. There are no seats, but the floor is always covered in carpet or prayer mats. When Muslims pray, they always face towards the holy city of Makkah. So a mosque usually has a small arch in one wall to show the direction of Makkah. There is also a raised part of the floor at one end of the mosque, at the top of a few steps.

A mosque in Birmingham

Inside a mosque in London

This is used by the **imam** when he talks to everyone at prayers on a Friday. The imam is a leader who is chosen by all the other Muslims at the mosque. They choose him because they respect him and because he knows the Qur'an very well.

New words

dome part of the roof of a building, shaped like half a ball
imam leader of Muslims
masjid Arabic name for mosque
minaret tall tower of a mosque
mosque Muslim place of worship

Other uses for a mosque

As well as being used for lunchtime prayers on a Friday, mosques are used for prayers every day. Men try to go to the mosque as often as they can.

Mosques are used as meeting places for people as well as for worship. In countries where not everyone is a Muslim, it is important to have somewhere to meet.

The mosque is also used as a school, where young people can be taught Arabic and the Qur'an. This is important for Muslims living in countries where children may not learn a lot about Islam at school during the day. Many mosques have rooms where a visitor can stay, and canteens where they can eat. They may also have study rooms and libraries.

13

The five pillars of Islam

This section is about the most important things that Muslims believe.

A pillar is something solid which supports a building. The five pillars of Islam are not real pillars. They are things that Muslims believe. They are called pillars because following what they say 'supports' Islam. Keeping the five pillars helps Muslims keep their religion properly.

The first pillar
The first pillar is accepting the most important things that Muslims believe. The simplest way of putting this is called the **shahadah**.

In English, it says 'There is no other God but Allah, and Muhammad is the prophet of Allah'. These words are very important. Muslims say them when they wake up in the morning, and before they go to sleep at night, and at every prayer.

The second pillar
The second pillar is praying five times a day. Muslims pray in the morning, three times during the day and at night. When it is time for prayer, Muslims stop what they are doing, and face in the direction of Makkah. They need to be in a clean place to pray, but they do not have to be in a mosque.

The five pillars

FAITH   PRAYER   ALMS   FASTING   PILGRIMAGE

14

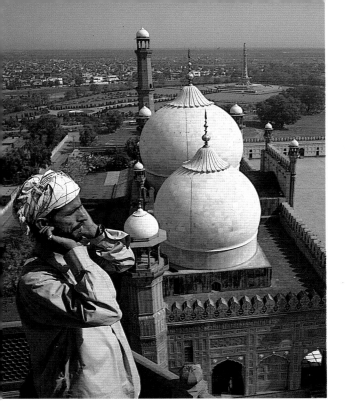

A mu'adhin

The mu'adhin

The mu'adhin is a man who calls Muslims to prayer. Muslims pray five times a day, and it is the mu'adhin's job to make sure that all Muslims know that it is time for prayer.

Years ago, all mu'adhins stood at the top of the minaret. Some still do, like in the photo on this page. Many mosques now have loudspeakers. This means that the mu'adhin can be heard more clearly. He repeats the call to prayer, which says 'God is the greatest. There is no God but Allah. Muhammad is the prophet of Allah. Come to prayer, come to security, Allah is most great!'

The third pillar

The third pillar is giving money to people who are poor or in need. Muslims believe it is their duty to Allah and to other Muslims to give some of their money every year.

The fourth pillar

The fourth pillar is **fasting**. For a month every year, Muslims do not eat or drink at all during the daytime. This is described in more detail on pages 22–23.

The fifth pillar

The fifth pillar is called Hajj. This is **pilgrimage** to Makkah. Hajj is described in more detail on pages 18–21.

How Muslims pray

This section tells you about how Muslims pray.

When do Muslims pray?
Prayer is the most important part of Muslim worship. Muslims pray five times a day. The times are written in the Qur'an. The first time is between first light and when the sun rises. The second time is after noon when the sun is highest. The third time is between mid-afternoon and sunset. The fourth time is after sunset but before it is dark. The fifth time for prayer is while it is dark.

When Muslims pray, they always face in the direction of Makkah. In a mosque, part of the wall shows where Makkah is. When they are travelling, many Muslims carry a special compass so they can work out where Makkah is from anywhere in the world. Muslims often use a prayer mat to kneel on.

Wudu
Before they pray, Muslims wash. This special washing is called **wudu**. It has nothing to do with being dirty.

Wudu makes the person more fit to talk to Allah, who is holy. It also gives Muslims a time when they can forget what they have been doing, and get ready to think only about Allah.

Prayers
Muslims do not just make up their prayers. These follow a set pattern. The pattern is called a **rak'ah**. The number of rak'ahs in the prayers changes at different times of the day.

There are nine movements in a rak'ah. As Muslims begin to pray, they stand. Then they bow, kneel and touch the ground with their forehead. Different parts of the prayer are said in each position.

Wudu is the special washing before prayer.

The first prayer position

The position for private prayers

Wudu

Wudu is the washing before prayer. The way in which Muslims should wash is written in the Qur'an. They always wash in the same order, so that they do not forget anything.

In the prayers, Muslims thank Allah that they can worship him. They pray for Muhammad and Muslims everywhere. In the last movement, they turn their head from side to side. This is to remember the two invisible angels that Muslims believe are always with every person.

Private prayers
When they have finished the rak'ah, Muslims can add prayers of their own. They usually stay kneeling on the floor. Private prayers can be made at any time, not just after a rak'ah.

First they wash the right hand, then the left hand, then the mouth and throat (by gargling). The voice must be clean, because it will be used to talk to Allah. Then the nose and face are washed, and the right arm, then the left. The head and ears are wiped with a wet hand. Last of all, the feet and ankles are washed, right one first. If there is no water for washing, the Qur'an says that you may touch clean sand or earth and copy the movements for washing hands, face and arms.

The Hajj (1)

This section tells you about how Muslims get ready to go on a pilgrimage to Makkah.

Hajj is the pilgrimage to Makkah. Every Muslim who is in good health and has enough money is expected to go to Makkah at least once in their life. Many Muslims save up for years to get enough money. Sometimes families join together to pay for one person to go.

When does Hajj take place?

To be a proper Hajj, the journey to Makkah must be made in the last month of the Muslim year. This is called the month of Dhul-Hijjah. A person making Hajj should be in Makkah between the 8th and the 13th of the month.

A person making a pilgrimage is called a pilgrim. About 2 million pilgrims go to Makkah to make Hajj. Only Muslims are allowed to go to Makkah.

The pilgrim camp

Worship

What do pilgrims wear?

Women always wear simple clothes. Men all wear exactly the same. They have two sheets of white cotton. One sheet is wrapped around the lower part of their body. The other goes over their left shoulder. The clothes are called **ihram**. This is also the word for the way pilgrims live while they are on Hajj. Wearing exactly the same clothes shows that Allah cares for everyone. It does not matter if they are rich or poor.

Why do people make Hajj?

Going to Makkah for Hajj is one of the most important things in a Muslim's life. They can worship with millions of other Muslims. But the point of Hajj is that each person does it for themselves. Muslims believe that if someone makes Hajj in the right way, Allah will forgive them for everything they have done wrong in their life.

Pilgrims wearing ihram

Ihram

While they are on Hajj, pilgrims try to live especially good lives, and not harm any living thing. They are expected not to swear or quarrel with anybody. Even if husbands and wives are both on Hajj, they are not allowed to sleep together.

Everybody tries to live as simply as possible. No one wears jewellery or perfume. People wear only open sandals on their feet. Women cover their heads. Men must be bare-headed, but they can carry an umbrella to protect them from the sun. No one cuts their hair or their nails while they are on Hajj.

New word

ihram the special way pilgrims live while they are on Hajj. Also the word used for the clothes that they wear

19

The Hajj (2)

This section tells you about how Muslims make Hajj.

The Ka'bah

The **Ka'bah** is the first place pilgrims go when they get to Makkah. The Ka'bah is a building shaped like a cube. Muslims believe that it was the first place on earth where Allah was worshipped.

Inside the Ka'bah is a room covered with writings from the Qur'an. Outside, the Ka'bah is covered in a black cloth with beautiful embroidery on it. At the end of each Hajj, this cloth is cut up and pilgrims take pieces of it home with them.

Pilgrims at the Ka'bah

Every pilgrim walks round the Ka'bah seven times. Those who are close enough may touch it once each time. Other pilgrims raise their hands towards it. Then the pilgrims go to pray nearby. After that they hurry seven times between two small hills near the Ka'bah. This remembers how Ibrahim's wife ran between the two hills looking for water for her baby. Pilgrims drink water from the well that she found.

The wuquf

The most important part of the Hajj is the **wuquf**. This means 'stand before Allah'. Pilgrims travel to the Plain of Arafat. They stand from midday until sunset, thinking about Allah.

The corridor between the two hills

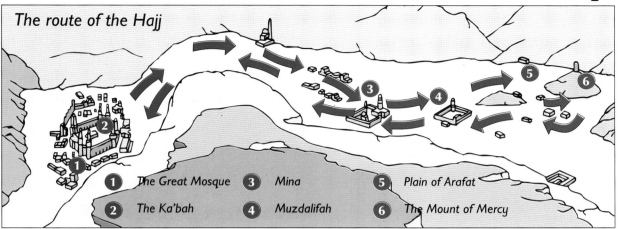

The route of the Hajj

1 The Great Mosque
2 The Ka'bah
3 Mina
4 Muzdalifah
5 Plain of Arafat
6 The Mount of Mercy

They pray and ask Allah to forgive them for all their **sins** (wrong things in their life).

Id-ul-Adha

Id-ul-Adha is part of a festival which takes place all over the world (see page 25). For Muslims on Hajj, it is special.

After Id-ul-Adha, the pilgrims camp at a place called Mina for three more days. Then they travel back to Makkah. They walk around the Ka'bah again, and drink water from the well.

New words

Ka'bah most important place of worship for Muslims

sins wrong things which someone has done

wuquf 'stand before Allah' – the most important part of the Hajj

When they have done this, the Hajj is ended, and they may travel home. Some pilgrims visit other important places nearby.

The Well of Zamzam

The Well of Zamzam is in the courtyard of the Great Mosque in Makkah. Muslims believe that this well was shown to Ibrahim's wife, Hajar, by the Angel Jibril. For Muslims, this makes the water very important.

When they are on Hajj, they drink as much water from it as they can. Many pilgrims take water home for friends and relations. Some pilgrims dip their white clothes in it, and take them home to be used as the cloth in which their body will be wrapped when they die.

Ramadan

This section tells you about an important month for Muslims.

Every year during the Muslim month of Ramadan, Muslims fast for the hours of daylight. This means they do not eat or drink anything. Muslims believe that this is very important.

Why do Muslims fast?
Muslims fast because Allah said in the Qur'an that they should. It is a way of showing that they are living their lives in the way Allah wants.

Muslim men praying at a mosque

Muslims believe it shows that their religion is the most important thing in their lives. They also believe that it shows everyone is equal. Hunger is the same for everyone, no matter whether they are rich or poor.

Who fasts?
Ramadan is not easy, but it should not be cruel. So some people do not have to fast. Children under the age of seven do not fast. Older children do not usually fast as strictly as grown-ups. Anyone who is on a journey is allowed to eat, but they are expected to make up the days they have missed later.

Pregnant women are not expected to fast, nor is anyone who is ill. Some people may never be able to fast, because they have an illness where fasting could be dangerous for them. They are expected to give money to the poor, instead.

What happens if Muslims do not fast?
There are no set punishments for anyone who does not fast. Muslims believe that it is up to each person to do what is right.

A Muslim family breaking their fast

They believe that Allah expects people to fast, and not to do so is cheating him. Muslims believe that at the end of the world, there will be a **Day of Judgement**. Allah will judge everyone on how they have lived, and each person will get what they deserve.

How do Muslims know when they can eat?

Tables are published with lists of the times in different places when the sun rises and sets during Ramadan, so that people know when to stop eating. They usually have a meal before dawn, then eat nothing until the sun sets, when they have a light snack. A main meal follows after the evening prayer.

How to live during Ramadan

Fasting is one part of Ramadan, but there are other things that make it special, too. During Ramadan, Muslims try to live especially good lives. They read the Qur'an more, and may go to the mosque every evening for special prayers.

During the last ten days of Ramadan, some Muslims go and live in the mosque. They take just a few necessary things with them, and live as simply as they can. They spend all their time reading the Qur'an, praying and thinking about Allah and how they should live. This is how Muhammad spent the last part of Ramadan when he was alive, so Muslims believe that they are following his example.

Id-ul-Fitr and Id-ul-Adha

This section tells you about two important Muslim festivals.

Id-ul-Fitr

Id-ul-Fitr is the festival at the end of Ramadan. Ramadan is the month when Muslims fast, and they look forward to Id-ul-Fitr very much. Before the festival begins, Muslims give money to the poor. Giving money to the poor is one of the five pillars of Islam, and at Id-ul-Fitr the idea is that everyone should have enough money to be able to celebrate the festival.

Gifts for Id-ul-Fitr

Some Muslims send cards at Id-ul-Fitr

The festival begins when the new moon appears in the sky. This shows that the new month has begun. Many people do not go to bed that night. They go outside with friends watching for the new moon. Then they meet for prayers and parties.

The festival begins with a meal. In the morning everyone goes to the mosque. There are prayers, when everyone thanks Allah that they have been able to fast.

After the prayers, people meet family and friends at home. Many Muslims celebrate Id with parties, especially for children. People often give each other presents and cards.

Id-ul-Adha

Id-ul-Adha is two months after Id-ul-Fitr. It is celebrated by Muslims all over the world, but it is most important for Muslims who are on Hajj at Makkah. At this time, Muslims remember the story in the Qur'an about how Ibrahim almost **sacrificed** his son Isma'il so that his life could be given to Allah. Just in time, Ibrahim heard a voice telling him not to do this. He had proved that he would obey Allah, and killing his son was not necessary. Ibrahim killed a ram instead, and this was the beginning of the festival.

At Id-ul-Adha, Muslims sacrifice or share in the sacrifice of a sheep or a goat. Prayers are said as the animal is killed, so that its life is given to Allah. Muslims say that this is a sign that they are ready to give up everything for Allah. Id-ul-Adha is a more serious festival than Id-ul-Fitr.

New word

sacrifice killing something so that its life can be offered to a god

Ibrahim and Isma'il

This story is in the Qur'an. Ibrahim had a son, Isma'il, whom he loved very much. One night, Ibrahim dreamt that Allah wanted him to sacrifice Isma'il. In those days, people believed that dreams were often messages from a god. Ibrahim and Isma'il both believed that they should obey the dream, even though they did not understand why Allah could want this. Just as Ibrahim was about to kill his son, he heard a voice telling him to stop, and kill a ram instead.

Ibrahim had shown how much he loved Allah. He loved him enough to give up the thing that was most important to him because he believed it was what Allah wanted. Muslims believe this story shows what real love of Allah is like.

Other festivals

This section tells you about three days in the year which are important for Muslims.

The Day of the Hijrah

The day of the Hijrah is on the first day of the month of Muharram.

Muharram is the first month in the Muslim year, so it is New Year's Day in the Muslim calendar. It is important for another reason, too. It is the day when Muslims remember the Hijrah, the journey which Muhammad made from Makkah to Madinah.

The Dome of the Rock mosque in Jerusalem

This was the real beginning of the success of Islam. On this day, many Muslims make promises that they will live a better life in the year to come. They believe that this means they are making a journey in their life, like the one that Muhammad made from Makkah to Madinah.

The Night of Power
This festival remembers the night when Muhammad was given the first part of the Qur'an by the Angel Jibril. It falls in the month of Ramadan. Many Muslims celebrate it on 27 Ramadan. Muslims spend time reading the Qur'an.

The Night of the Journey
The Night of the Journey is celebrated on the 27th day of the month of Rajab. Muslims believe that on that day an amazing thing happened to Muhammad. In one day, he made a journey from Makkah to Jerusalem! (Look at the map on page 4.) Jerusalem is a very important city in the religions of Islam, Judaism and Christianity. From Jerusalem, Muhammad was taken up to heaven. He heard Allah teaching about how important it is to pray five times a day. Then he was carried back to Makkah. Some Muslims believe that this was a vision which Muhammad had.

Celebrating festivals

Muslim festivals are usually quite serious, because they remember important events in the history of Islam. However, they are also Muslim holidays and a chance for Muslims to enjoy themselves. They are a time for giving presents and wearing new clothes. At Id-ul-Fitr, children are given presents of sweets, nuts and money.

Sugared almonds and other sweets, beautifully wrapped in boxes with ribbons, are a traditional present. People visiting friends and relations at festival times take small presents with them. Almost all Muslims meet their friends and relations and share special meals together. This helps to make the festivals a time that everyone can enjoy.

The history of Islam

This section tells you something about the history of Islam after Muhammad died.

After Muhammad died, other men took over as leaders of Islam. At first there were problems, because when Muhammad died there were quarrels among the Muslims.

Some people left Islam. Others began to think that anyone who did not share their own point of view was wrong.

The new leaders had to fight to defend Islam and make it stronger. Fighting to defend Islam is called **jihad**.

Within a hundred years of Muhammad's death, Muslims ruled large parts of the world. They went to India, where they ruled until the nineteenth century. They ruled parts of northern Africa, Spain and Eastern Europe.

In the Middle Ages, one area was fought over more than others. This was the land called Palestine, at the eastern end of the Mediterranean Sea. It was important to Muslims, but it was important to Christians and Jews, too. All three religions believe that the city of Jerusalem is holy, and all three wanted to control it.

Where Muslims ruled in 732 CE

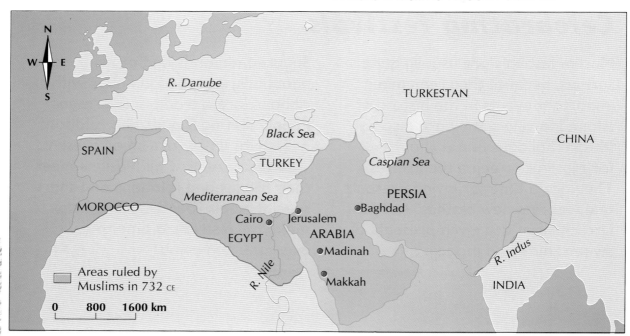

Areas ruled by Muslims in 732 CE

0   800   1600 km

The Alhambra in Spain was built by Muslims.

Other ways in which Islam spread

Islam did not just spread by fighting. For hundreds of years, many Muslims were traders. They travelled all over the world buying and selling things.

People saw that Muslims lived good lives. They began to think that Islam must be a good religion.

Sometimes they decided to become Muslims themselves.

Today, there are about 1000 million Muslims in the world. There are Muslims in almost every country. Islam is growing faster than any other religion.

New word
Jihad to struggle against evil

Jihad

Jihad means 'to struggle against evil'. Muslims believe that fighting is not wrong if it is necessary to put something right. Jihad has become an important part of Muslim belief, so it has been very important in Muslim history. Jihad does not mean that any battle in which Muslims fight is right. There are strict rules in the Qur'an which say whether or not a battle can be called jihad.

For example, it must only be fought to defend Islam, not to take over another country. It must be to try to get back to a time of peace. It must be led by a leader of Islam. Fighting must stop as soon as enemy soldiers give up their weapons. Women and children cannot be included in the war, and battles must be fought without damaging crops and trees.

Muslim groups

This section tells you something about the two main groups of Muslims.

While Muhammad was alive, he was the Muslim leader. When he died, all the Muslims agreed that they needed a new leader. They agreed one of Muhammad's closest friends should be the new leader.

The main choice was between Muhammad's father-in-law Abu Bakr, and his son-in-law Ali. Abu Bakr was chosen. When he died, a second leader was chosen. When the second leader died, a third leader was chosen, and when he died, a fourth.

The fourth leader was Ali, Muhammad's son-in-law.

After these four leaders, quarrels began. Some Muslims thought that Ali should have been the first leader, followed by his son, and so on. There were more and more arguments between the group who believed this and the other Muslims.

At last, the Muslims who wanted Ali's family to be the leaders split away from the other Muslims. They became the group that today we call Shi'a Muslims. Shi'ah comes from an Arabic word which means 'separate party'.

Countries where more than half the people are Muslim

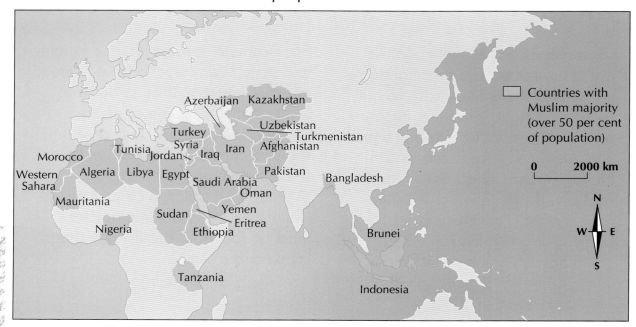

Azerbaijan Kazakhstan
Uzbekistan
Turkey Turkmenistan
Tunisia Syria Iran Afghanistan
Morocco Jordan Iraq
Western Algeria Libya Egypt Pakistan Bangladesh
Sahara Saudi Arabia
Mauritania Oman
Sudan Yemen
Nigeria Eritrea
Ethiopia Brunei
Tanzania
Indonesia

Countries with Muslim majority (over 50 per cent of population)

0   2000 km

N W E S

Shi'ah Muslims

Shi'ah Muslims
About one in ten Muslims in the world today belongs to the Shi'ah group. Most Shi'ahs live in the countries called Iran and Iraq. They are very strict about what they believe.

Sometimes they are ready to fight and give up their lives for their beliefs. Someone who dies for what they believe is called a **martyr**. Islam teaches that martyrs will go straight to Allah and live in **Paradise**.

New words
Ayatollah leader of Shi'ah Muslims
martyr someone who dies for what they believe
Paradise garden of happiness for life after death

Sunni Muslims
When the Shi'ah Muslims split away, a much bigger group was left behind. This group are called Sunni Muslims. Sunni comes from a word which means 'authority'. About nine in every ten Muslims today belong to this group. Sunni Muslims think that they are the ones who really follow Muhammad's teaching.

Shi'ah Muslim teachers

All Muslim teachers are called imams. Shi'ah Muslims believe that there were twelve imams who were special. They were all from the family of Muhammad. They believe that the first of these imams was Ali, who they say was chosen by Muhammad. His power was passed down to his son, and from father to son, until the twelfth imam.

This imam disappeared in 880 CE, but Shi'ah Muslims believe he will come back one day. Until that day, special teachers lead the Shi'ah Muslims. These leaders are called **Ayatollahs**.

The influence of Islam

This section tells you about some of the ways in which Muslims have changed the world.

Muslims believe that Allah made the world and everything in it. So they believe that it is important to understand the world and make the most of it.

Hundreds of years ago, people from many countries went to study at famous universities in Muslim cities. Muslim leaders always taught their people that they should learn as much as they can about the world. Many of the things which Muslims discovered and invented were not found in other countries for hundreds of years.

Numbers

When Muslims are travelling, they need to be able to work out which direction to face so that they can look towards Makkah when they pray. They also need to be able to work out the right times for prayers. This means that Muslims have always been interested in mathematics and and in studying the stars to find directions.

The most common way of counting – 1,2,3 – came first from Muslims, and so did many of the rules that we use in mathematics today.

Medicine

Muslim doctors discovered that plants, especially the plants we call herbs, could be used to help people who were ill.

They found a way of putting people to sleep for operations, so that they did not feel the pain. They were the first people to discover the way that blood moves around the body. These discoveries were so important that doctors all over the world copied the ideas.

An old compass and sundial

Many Muslim buildings are very beautiful.

Being clean

Muhammad taught his friends that it was important to keep their bodies clean, because Allah made them. So Muslim leaders made sure that people in their towns and cities had clean water to drink and wash in.

Houses had clean water brought in pipes, and drains took dirty water and rubbish away.

It was hundreds of years before countries like Britain began to copy these ideas.

Did you know?

Many words and ideas that we use today were begun by Muslims. It was because of Muslims that paper began to be used in Europe. Before this, people used to write on animal skins. In everyday life, we all use words which began as Arabic words. Caravan, mattress and jacket began as Arabic words.

So did apricot, coffee and sugar. Even people who know very little about Islam use ideas and words which were begun by Muslims. Knowing more about how these things began helps people to realize that as well as being a religion, Islam has been an important way of life for hundreds of years.

Art in Islam

This section tells you a little about the way art is used in Islam.

Why is the art in Islam special?

Muslims do not use pictures of animals or people anywhere where worship may take place. This is because they believe that only Allah can make living things, and it is wrong to try to copy Allah. Muhammad had many battles with people in Makkah who were worshipping statues and pictures. He was afraid that people might worship them instead of Allah.

What do Muslim artists draw?

Muslim artists usually draw plants and flowers. Often they draw beautiful patterns. These patterns are used for decorating buildings like mosques and houses, and in cloth, rugs and cushions. Muslims are famous for making beautiful carpets.

Weaving

Many Muslims have become very good at making cloth or rugs and blankets. This is because years ago many Muslims used to live in tents, travelling from place to place.

Patterns are used to make buildings look beautiful.

This was to find grass and water in the desert for their animals. They used rugs and cushions for furniture because they were easier to pack up and move than beds and chairs.

Calligraphy

Calligraphy is the name for writing which is so beautiful that it becomes a pattern itself.

Calligraphy began when Muslims were copying the Qur'an. Because they thought it was so important, they wanted the writing to look as beautiful as possible. They began making patterns out of the writing.

Calligraphy – this is part of the Qur'an.

Favourite words for patterns are verses from the Qur'an and the name of Allah. Calligraphy is often used for decorations, too.

New word

calligraphy writing done so that it becomes a decoration

Prayer mats

Prayer mats are the mats which Muslims often use when they pray. They are one of the things in which Muslim art can be seen.

Many prayer mats have beautiful patterns on them in bright colours. Sometimes there is also a picture of a place which is important for Muslims. For example, the Ka'bah in Makkah. No prayer mat ever has a picture of an animal or person. Muslims believe that this would be wrong.

Often the pattern or the picture is arranged so that it points towards the top of the prayer mat. This helps Muslims to make sure that they are facing towards Makkah when they pray.

The Muslim family

This section tells you something about the way Muslim families live.

Family life

Family life is very important to Muslims. Muslims believe that the idea of a family came from Allah. Being a member of a happy family is an important part of being a Muslim.

Extended families

Many Muslims live with or very close to grandparents, uncles and aunts in an **extended family**. This means that cousins can often be loved and thought of in the same way as brothers and sisters.

Children are seen as being a gift from Allah, and Islam teaches that parents have duties to a child.

A Muslim family

Grandparents are important members of the family.

New word

extended family family which has grandparents, cousins, and other relatives living as one family

The parents' first duty is to choose a name for the child. They have a duty to bring the child up carefully, and to follow Islam. The child should be educated as well as possible, so that they are able to support their family when they grow up.

The parents' duties also include helping their son or daughter find someone suitable to marry when they grow up.

Islam teaches that children have duties to their parents, too. Just as parents look after their children when they are young and cannot care for themselves, children should look after their parents when they are old. This means that older relations should be treated with great respect, even if they become confused or ill.

The whole Muslim family

Islam teaches that all Muslims are members of one big family. This is called the Ummah. This idea is very important for Muslims. They believe that Allah made everyone, and everyone is equal. This means that we should all care about everyone, no matter what colour skin they have, where they live or what language they speak.

So Muslims are often very interested and concerned about what is happening to other Muslims, even when they live in parts of the world which are far away.

Women in Islam

This section tells you something about women in Islam.

At the time when Muhammad was alive, women were often treated badly. Many women were just servants for men.

Muhammad said that this was not right. Women should be cared for and respected. Islam allows women to own things. They have the same rights as men when they need to make decisions that involve them. Remember that in many Eastern countries, where Islam began, women were and still are very protected.

Male relations would be expected to act for them in anything that was important.

Marriage

Muslim men and women are expected to marry. It is usual for the marriage to be **arranged** (see page 43).

Muslim law says that a woman should not be made to marry if she does not want to. She can keep any money or property which she owned before the marriage, and any money which she earns while she is married. A Muslim woman does not take her husband's surname.

This Muslim woman is a doctor.

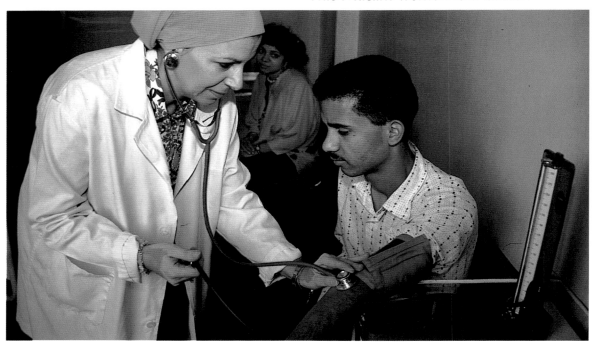

Muslim girls reading the Qur'an.

People

This includes their legs and arms. When they are outside the home or with people they do not know, many women choose to wear clothes that show as little of their body as possible. They wear a dress that covers them to their feet, and a scarf or veil over their head. This is called **hijab**. The women in the picture on page 31 are dressed in hijab.

Work

Many Muslims believe that it is a man's job to go out and earn money, and a woman's job to look after the home. These jobs are seen as different but just as important as each other. However, it is now more common for Muslim women to work outside the home.

Clothes

Muslims think that women should dress decently. Short skirts and tight clothes are not allowed in Islam. Muslim women should always keep their body covered.

Women in the mosque

Muslim women are expected to follow the same teachings as men. The only difference in the way they follow Islam is that they are not expected to go to the mosque, even on a Friday, when the men should go. Women usually stay at home with their children. They still pray in the same way.

When women do go to the mosque, they pray either in a different room, or at the back of the main room. Muslims believe that this means that everyone can concentrate on Allah while they pray.

New words

arranged marriage marriage where relatives find out if a person is suitable

hijab the clothes worn by Muslim women

Islam in the home

This section tells you a little about how Muslims live at home.

Muslims believe that their religion affects everything they do in their lives, because they should obey Allah in everything. This means that the way they live is very important.

Food

Like many religions, Islam teaches that not all foods are allowed. Food which Muslims are allowed to eat is called **halal**. Fish are halal, and so are all fruit and vegetables.

For meat to be halal, the animal must be killed in a special way. Muslims have their own butchers so that they can eat meat like beef, lamb and chicken.

Anything which comes from a pig cannot be halal. Neither can anything from an animal which eats other animals. If an animal is not killed so that it is halal, anything which comes from it is not allowed. This includes the fat from the animal.

Many other foods contain animal fat, like biscuits, cakes and some cheeses.

Learning about Islam at home

Muslims should only eat halal food.

Muslims do not usually eat these unless they have been prepared with halal fat or vegetable oils.

Alcohol

Muslims should not drink alcohol, and it is forbidden in Muslim countries. It is not really enough for Muslims not to drink it themselves. They should not be anywhere near when alcohol is being drunk. For Muslims living in countries like Britain or Australia this can be a problem, because many people go to pubs and places which serve alcohol.

Smoking

Smoking is not forbidden, but Muslims are not supposed to smoke because it damages the body. Muslims believe that it is wrong to harm anything which Allah made.

New word

halal 'allowed' – food which Muslims can eat

Halal meat

For Muslims to be able to eat any part of an animal, it must be killed in a special way. Before it is killed, it must be treated kindly. Then it must be killed kindly. First, the animal is dedicated to Allah. This is to make it clear that the animal is being killed because it is necessary for food, and its life is being given back to Allah.

The animal's throat is cut quickly with a very sharp knife. It becomes unconscious through lack of blood before it feels pain. All the blood must be removed. Muslims believe that this is the kindest method possible of killing an animal.

Muslims in other countries

This section tells you something about how Muslims live in a country where most people are not Muslim.

There are about 2 million Muslims living in Britain, about 3 million in America and about 150,000 in Australia. Some Muslims are people whose families once lived in another country.

A Muslim family in Britain

Others are Muslim **converts** – people who have been impressed by the teachings of Islam, and have decided to become Muslims themselves.

Sometimes living in a country where most people are not Muslim can cause problems. Other people do not dress or behave in the way that Islam teaches is right.

Prayer
Muslims pray five times a day. They need somewhere clean, usually with somewhere to wash, too. This can be difficult if they are working somewhere where people do not understand.

Dress
Islam says that both men and women should dress decently. For men, this means being covered from the waist to the knees. For women, it means that only their hands and face should be seen.

Once they have reached the age of about twelve, girls are expected to keep their legs, head and arms covered.

Young Muslim girls keep their legs covered for PE.

In countries where girls do PE and swimming at school, this can cause difficulties.

Women who wear long clothes and veils over their heads are sometimes laughed at by people who do not understand.

At school
Once girls and boys get to the age of about twelve, Muslims prefer that they should not have lessons together. Boys and girls are not allowed to go out alone together. This can sometimes cause problems where young Muslims are mixing with non-Muslim friends.

New word
convert become a member of a religion

Arranged marriages

An arranged marriage is one where relations of a man or woman help them to find a suitable person to marry. The father of a woman finds out if a certain man would be a suitable husband for her. A man finds out about a woman suggested by his female relatives. Many young Muslims feel that this is a good idea, because their parents have had more experience of life.

In some families, however, there are problems. Young Muslims see their friends choosing boyfriends and girlfriends. They feel that they should be able to do the same. This is not forbidden in Islam, but boys and girls do not go out alone together.

Special occasions (1)

This section tells you about special things which happen to Muslim children.

Birth ceremonies

Muslims believe all children are a gift from Allah. When a baby is born, the call to prayer and the command to worship are whispered in its ear. So the first words the baby hears are the most important Muslim beliefs.

Sometimes a tiny piece of sugar or honey is placed on the baby's tongue. This is not part of the religion. No one knows why it is done. Some people think it is a way of showing that they hope the baby will be 'sweet' – a good person.

Aqiqah

When the baby is seven days old, the **aqiqah** ceremony is held. Years ago, a sheep or goat was killed and some of the meat given to poor people. Today, people often choose to give some money instead.

At this ceremony, the baby is given its name. All Muslim names have a meaning. As part of the aqiqah ceremony, the baby's head is shaved. Olive oil is sometimes rubbed into the head. The hair which has been cut off is weighed, and money is given to the poor. This money is what the hair would have been worth if it had been made of silver. If the baby is born without any hair, money is still given.

The call to prayer is whispered to a new baby.

At the madrasah

The madrasah

The **madrasah** is a special school held at the mosque. Children learn to read and write in Arabic. They also learn parts of the Qur'an and the correct way to pray.

New words

aqiqah naming ceremony
madrasah school at the mosque which children go to from about the age of four

Names in Islam

Children may be called after someone in the family, or someone in Muhammad's family. A boy may be given one of the names which Muslims use for Allah, with Abd in front of it. This means 'servant' in Arabic, so it is a way of saying that the child will serve Allah.

When they have a child, Muslim parents often stop using their own names, and become known as the child's parents instead. For example, the father of a boy called Muhammad may be called Abu Muhammad, and his mother may be called Umm Muhammad.

Special occasions (2)

This section tells you about Muslim marriage and death ceremonies.

Marriage

A Muslim marriage is not a religious service. Before they marry, the two people work out rules for their marriage. These are written down, and when the couple have signed them, they have to obey them.

A Muslim wedding in India

When they marry, the husband should give his wife a gift of money. The Qur'an says that a man may have up to four wives, but only if he can treat them all with equal fairness. Before the Qur'an, men were allowed to marry as many women as they liked.

Today, most men have only one wife. Some men do marry a second wife, if the first one cannot have children, or if she becomes ill and needs someone to look after her. This can only happen if the first wife agrees. It cannot happen in countries like Britain or America, where it is against the law to be married to more than one person at the same time.

Divorce

Divorce is the ending of a marriage when the husband and wife are still alive. Islam does allow divorce, but it does not approve of it.

If a married couple are having problems, friends and relations try to help them sort things out. It can be seen as a disgrace to the families if there is a divorce.

A Muslim funeral in Spain

Death

When a Muslim dies, the body is washed and wrapped in white sheets. Sometimes the sheets are from the person's Hajj. Muslims prefer that this washing should be done by the relations.

Muslims are always buried, never **cremated**. If possible, the body is in contact with the earth rather than in a coffin. It is buried so that it faces Makkah. Funerals are simple, and if possible they take place on the day of death.

New words

cremate to burn a body after death

Hell place of punishment for life after death

What happens after death?

Muslims believe that after death there is a life that never ends. This life is a test, and there will be a Day of Judgement. Muslims believe that there are two angels who are always with every person, even though they are not usually seen. At the Day of Judgement, these angels will tell Allah how each person has behaved in their life. Allah will then judge what each person deserves.

Those who have lived a good life will go to Paradise. Paradise is described as a beautiful garden of peace with trees and flowers. Everyone will be happy. Those who did not obey Allah in their life on earth will go to **Hell**, where they will suffer for ever in scorching fire and hot winds.

Index